STRESS LESS COLOR-BY-NUMBER™
FLOWERS

75 COLORING PAGES FOR PEACE AND RELAXATION

Adamsmedia
Avon, Massachusetts

Published by
Adams Media, a division of F+W Media, Inc.
57 Littlefield Street, Avon, MA 02322. U.S.A.
www.adamsmedia.com

Contains material adapted from *The Everything® Stress Management Book* by Eve Adamson, copyright © 2002 by F+W Media, Inc., ISBN 10: 1-58062-578-9, ISBN 13: 978-1-58062-578-4.

ISBN 10: 1-5072-0128-1
ISBN 13: 978-1-5072-0128-2

Printed in the United States of America.

10 9 8 7 6 5 4 3 2 1

Cover images © irinarivoruchko/123RF, IULIIA ZUBKOVA/123RF.
Interior images © 123RF.

This book is available at quantity discounts for bulk purchases.
For information, please call 1-800-289-0963.

INTRODUCTION

Looking to relax? Want to feel more creative? Need more peace and quiet in your life?

If you're looking to get rid of all the extra stress in your life, just pick up a pencil, crayon, or marker and let *Stress Less Color-By-Number™ Flowers* help you manage your worries in a fun, easy, and therapeutic way.

Over the years, studies have shown that coloring allows your mind to concentrate solely on the task at hand, which brings you into a restful state similar to what you can achieve through meditation. When you allow yourself to focus on the creative artwork in front of you, your mind doesn't have room for all the anxiety and stress in your life. And when your mind relaxes, your body follows, by letting go of any tension and giving you a sense of peace and well-being.

Throughout the book, you'll find 75 black-and-white images depicting a variety of beautiful flowers that are just waiting to be colored in. And the beauty of these prints is that they've been numbered so you can achieve beautiful results without the worry of choosing the colors yourself. Refer to the insert's color palette to find the color that corresponds with each number. Any spaces that aren't numbered should remain white. You'll also find a fully colored version of each image on the insert pages in this book to give you a preview of the lovely picture you will create when you follow the number pattern exactly. But if you'd rather, let your own unique palette guide your hand and personalize your image.

So whether you're new to art therapy or have been embracing the fun of coloring for years, it's time to stress less and find your inner calm and creativity—one flower print at a time.

FLOWER 1

FLOWER 2

FLOWER 3

FLOWER 4

FLOWER 5

FLOWER 6

FLOWER 7

FLOWER 8

FLOWER 9

FLOWER 10

FLOWER 11

FLOWER 12

FLOWER 13

FLOWER 14

FLOWER 15

FLOWER 16

FLOWER 17

FLOWER 18

FLOWER 19

FLOWER 20

FLOWER 21

FLOWER 22

FLOWER 23

FLOWER 24

FLOWER 25

FLOWER 26

FLOWER 27

FLOWER 28

FLOWER 29

FLOWER 30

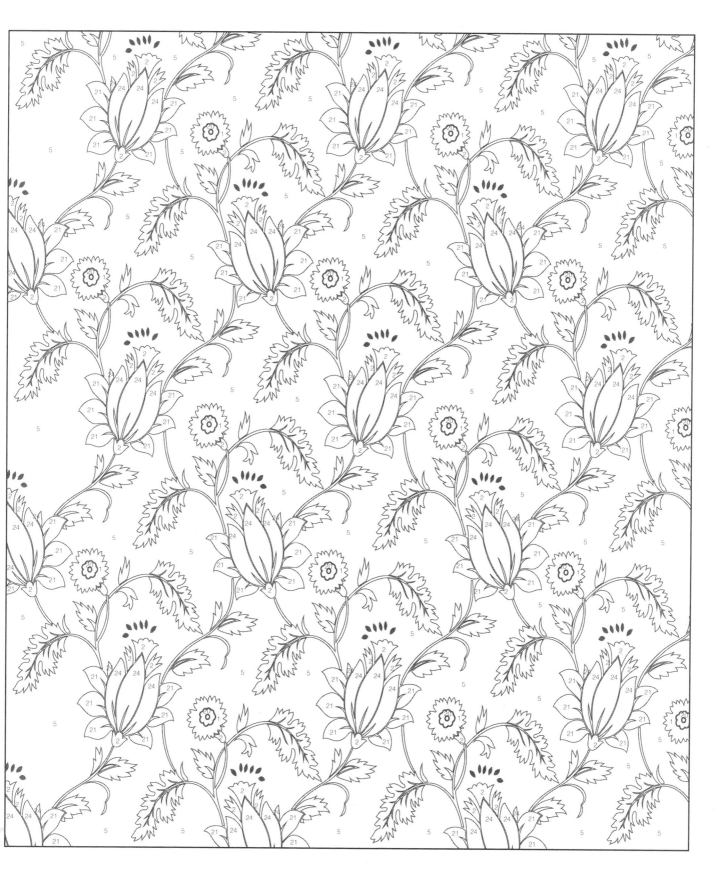

FLOWER 31

FLOWER 32

FLOWER 33

FLOWER 34

FLOWER 35

FLOWER 36

FLOWER 37

FLOWER 38

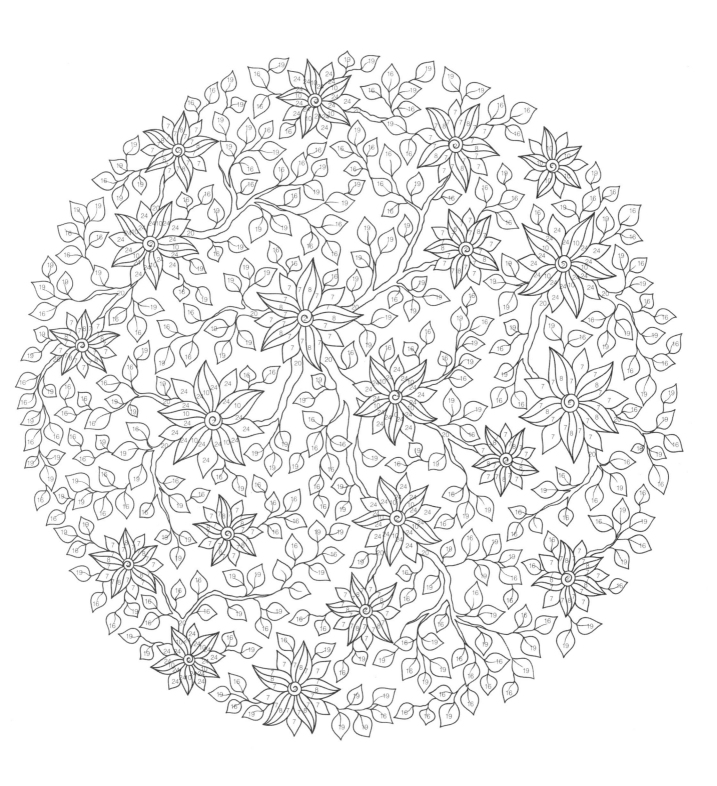

FLOWER 39

FLOWER 40

FLOWER 41

FLOWER 42

FLOWER 43

FLOWER 44

FLOWER 45

FLOWER 46

FLOWER 47

FLOWER 48

FLOWER 49

FLOWER 50

FLOWER 51

FLOWER 52

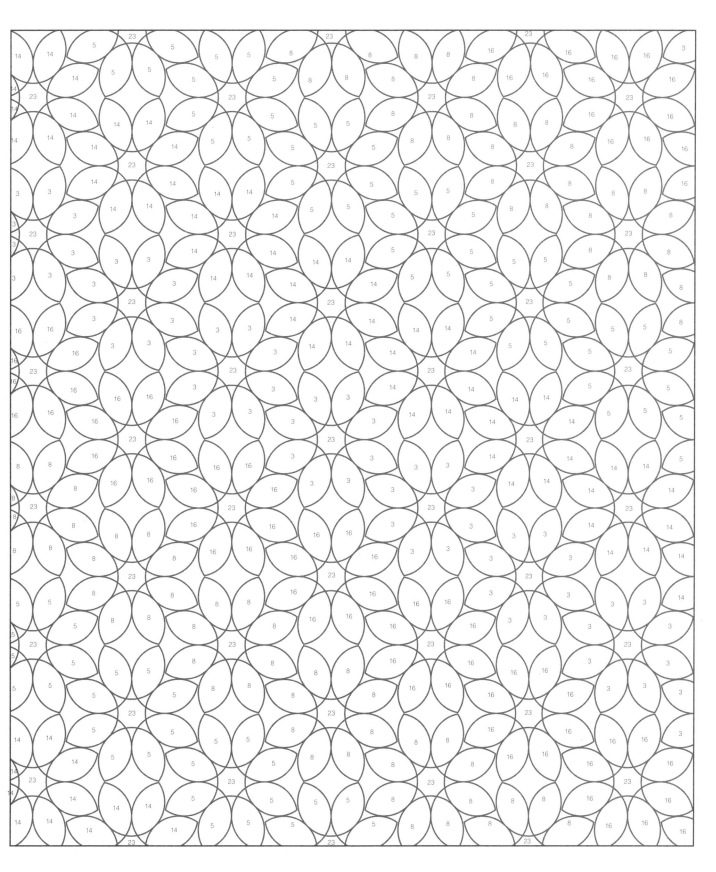

FLOWER 53

FLOWER 54

FLOWER 55

FLOWER 56

FLOWER 57

FLOWER 58

FLOWER 59

FLOWER 60

FLOWER 61

FLOWER 62

FLOWER 63

FLOWER 64

FLOWER 65

FLOWER 66

FLOWER 67

FLOWER 68

FLOWER 69

FLOWER 70

FLOWER 71

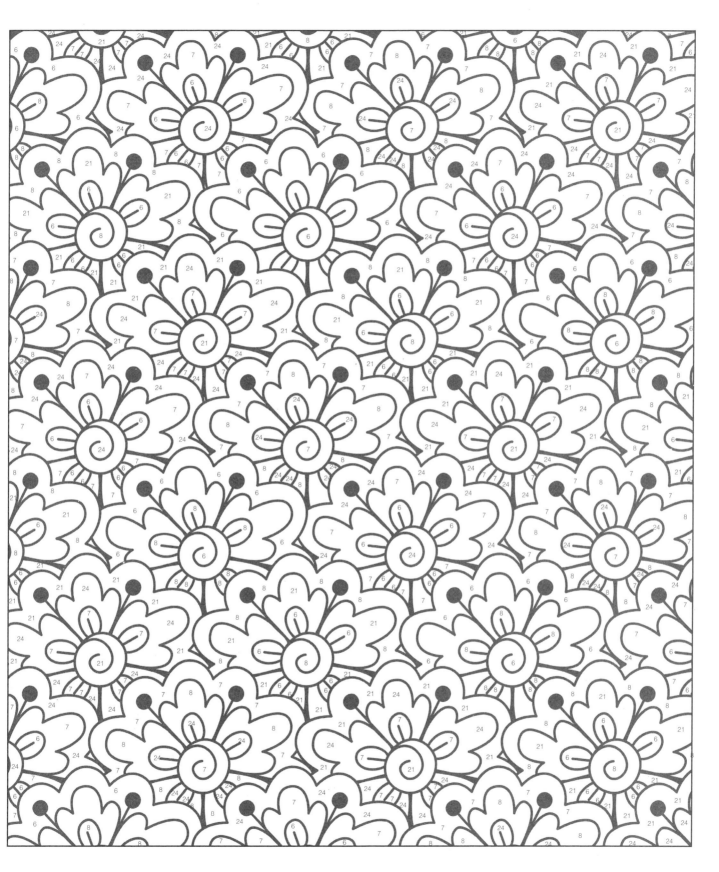

FLOWER 72

FLOWER 73

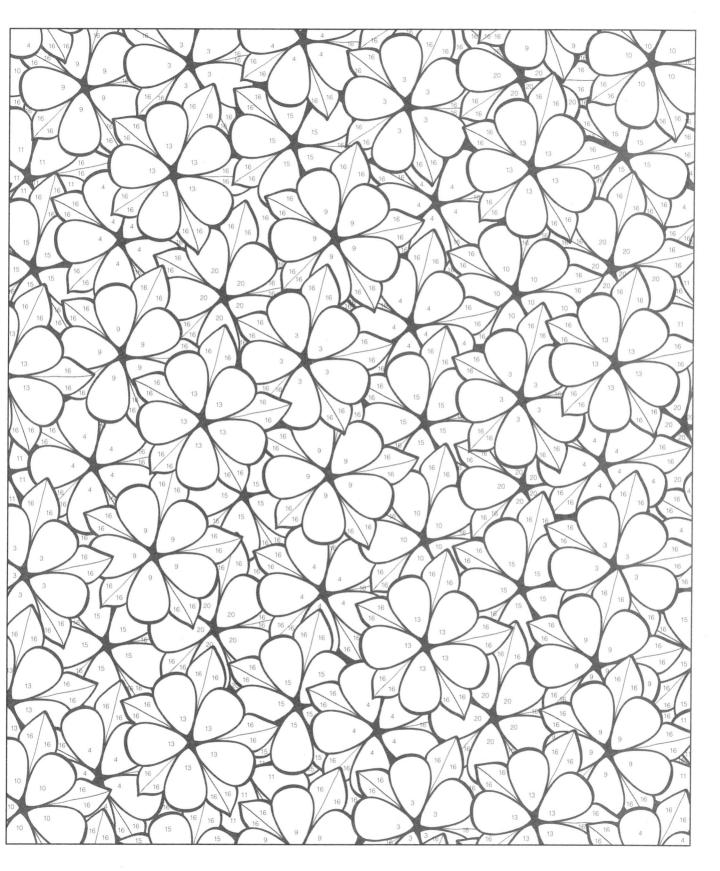

FLOWER 74

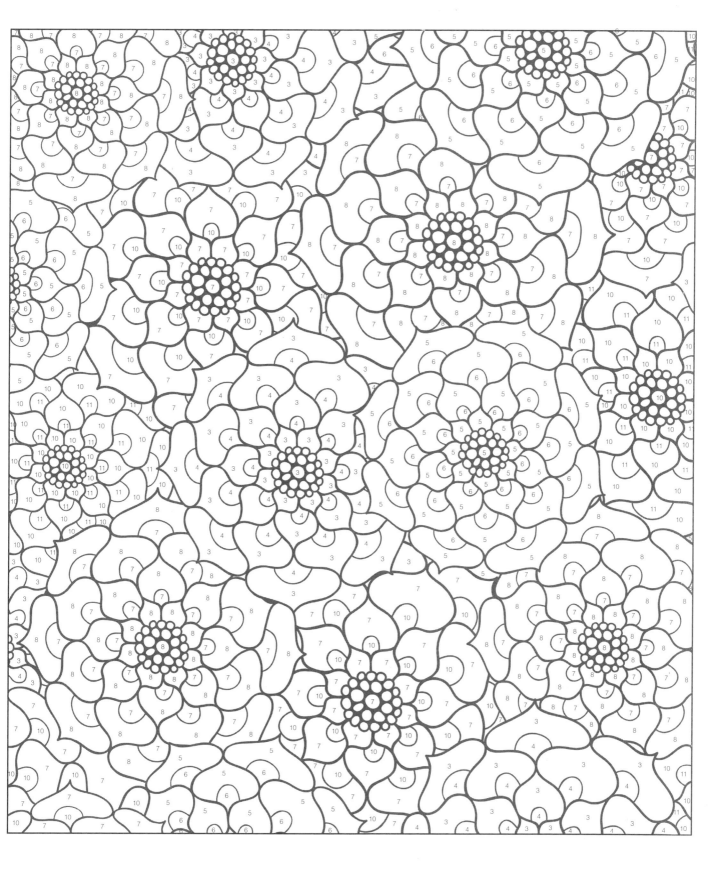

FLOWER 75

TEST PAGES

COLORED FLOWERS
REFERENCE GUIDE

COLOR KEY

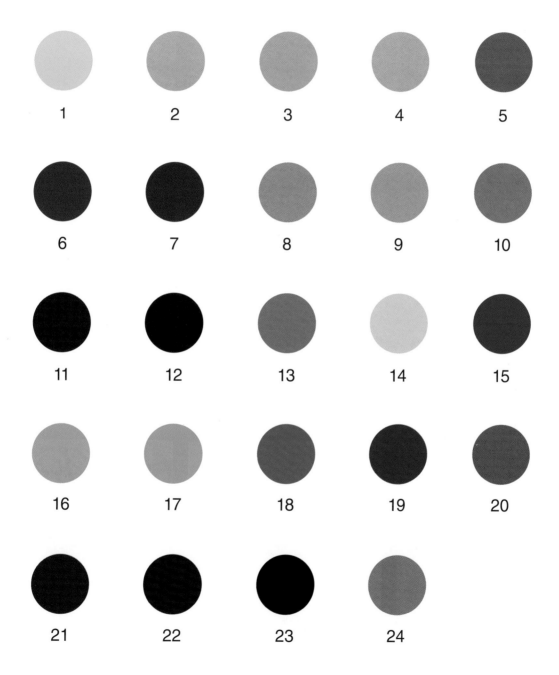

1

2

3

4

5

6

7

8

9

10

11

12

13

14

15

16

17

18

19

20

21

22

23

24

25

26

27

28

29

30

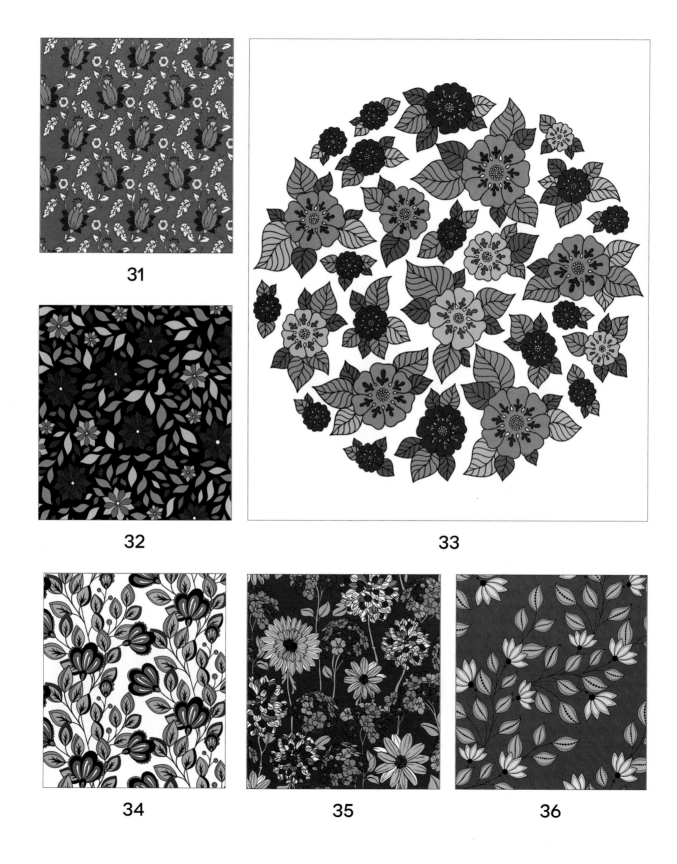

31

32

33

34

35

36

37

38

39

40

41

42

43

44

45

46

47

48

49

50

51

53

52

54

55

56

57

58

59

60

61

62

63

64

65

66

67

68

69

70

71

72

73

74

75